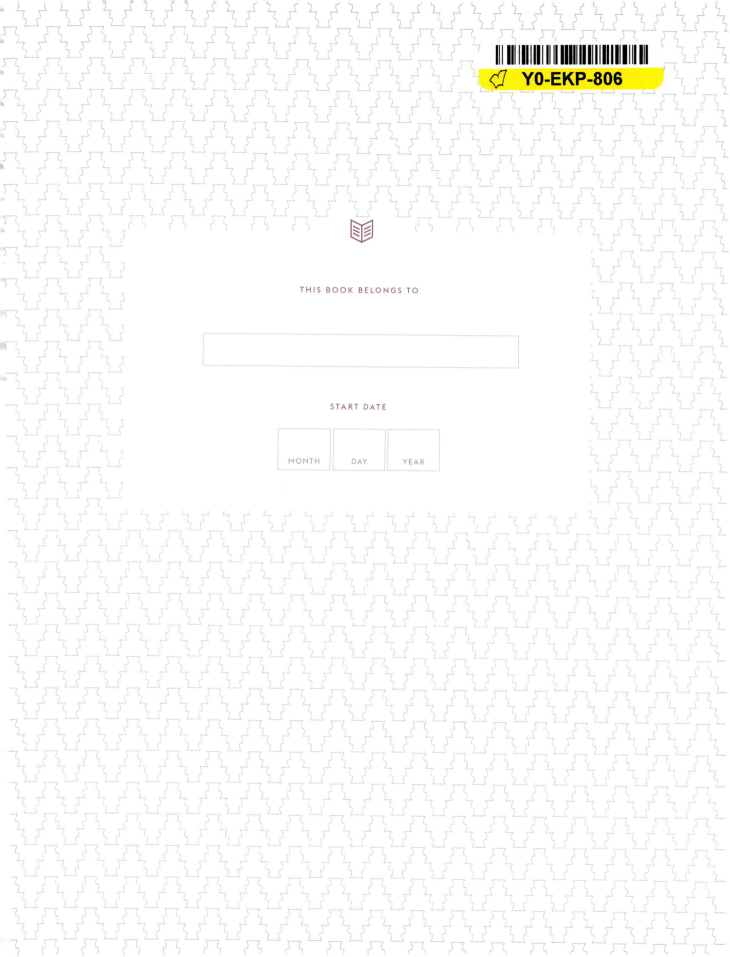

THIS BOOK BELONGS TO

START DATE

| MONTH | DAY | YEAR |

ESTHER

SHE READS TRUTH

Nashville, Tennessee

There's an old saying that goes, "When God closes a door, He opens a window." Perhaps you've heard it?

I believe God's work in the lives of His people is even more magnificent than that. The book of Esther supports this theory.

Even better than closing doors and opening windows, what we find in the book of Esther is the active, invisible, and preemptive hand of God at work in the most unexpected places. (I actually found myself laughing out loud at some of the startling plot twists and delightful ironies!)

Esther shows us that God does not go around simply reacting to whatever we throw at Him. He doesn't work that way. He acts first. God's invisible hand did not make a defensive move *after* Haman constructed a gallows on his front lawn. And God did not *pivot His plan* to react to Haman's decree to annihilate the Jewish people. Instead, His rescue plans were already in place—even before the danger began.

Esther was crowned queen of Persia well before it occurred to Haman to kill God's people. So when the danger came, she was already in the perfect position to act.

God's involvement in our lives is so much better than closed doors and open windows. In the story of Esther, and in our story of salvation,

God designs our deliverance even before man begins to devise our destruction.

This study of Esther is short and rich. In two weeks, it covers 10 chapters of an historical account of an actual king and a real kingdom. We've created some beautiful bonus spreads to help you study Old Testament feasts, sort out the characters in this story, and realize the stunning reversals in this plot, all pointing to the greatest reversal of all: Christ overcoming death by giving His own life. And as the cherry (or raspberry!) on top, we've included a fresh cookie recipe for you to bake and enjoy with your study group.

Read the book of Esther with us. Look for the active, invisible, preemptive hand of God. Consider the ways God has designed your own deliverance, and imagine the invisible ways He is caring for you even now.

God is good. And He is at work.

Raechel

Raechel Myers
EDITOR-IN-CHIEF

HOW TO STUDY WITH THE
ONLINE COMMUNITY

For added community, conversation, and devotionals, join us in the **Esther** reading plan on the She Reads Truth app or on SheReadsTruth.com—where women from New Haven to the Netherlands will be reading along with you!

Have a "He" in your life—a brother, father, husband, or friend? Invite him to join you by visiting HeReadsTruth.com or the He Reads Truth app, or by picking up the guy version of this book at ShopHeReadsTruth.com.

HOW TO USE THIS BOOK

She Reads Truth is a community of women dedicated to reading the Word of God every day.
The Bible is living and active, breathed out by God, and we confidently hold it higher than anything we
can do or say. This book focuses primarily on Scripture with helpful elements throughout.

SCRIPTURE READING

This study book includes daily Scripture readings, plus supplementary passages for fuller context.

JOURNALING SPACE

Each weekday offers space for personal reflection and prayer.

GRACE DAY

Use this day to catch up on your reading, pray, and rest in the presence of the Lord.

WEEKLY TRUTH

This day is set aside for weekly Scripture memorization.

"Our goal was to paint a broader picture, turning the spotlight from the story's heroine onto its Hero."

RYAN MYERS,
CREATIVE DIRECTOR

DESIGN ON PURPOSE

The book of Esther is a popular Old Testament read. It's not tough to find Bible studies based on this narrative, but the creative team at She Reads Truth enjoyed the challenge of putting their own aesthetic spin on an old favorite.

We decided not to depict a specific woman as Esther on the cover. Instead, we pulled a variety of photos from the She Reads Truth community and incorporated them throughout the book. Our goal was to paint a broader picture, turning the spotlight from the story's heroine onto its Hero. We aimed to remind the reader that the God who worked in Esther's life and used her for His purposes is the same God who cares for us as individuals today. Esther was one woman, but her God is Lord of all.

When Amanda of Amanda Christine Studio reached out to our creative team during an open call last spring, we excitedly filed her away in hopes of using her floral paintings for this very book, months down the road. We loved the way her rich magentas and purples nodded to this story's setting of Persian royalty and palace hijinks.

Even beyond the color pallette, Amanda's brush-stroke florals imagine the garden courtyard where so much of this story takes place. Think of these florals as the centerpieces at that 6-month-long festival thrown by King Ahasuerus (be still our event-planning hearts). Artwork—even something as seemingly simple as watercolor flowers—has the power to transport us.

One of the most important things to note about the design function of this book is that all of the daily Esther readings are pink instead of black. We did this purposefully, in order to set the primary text apart from the supplementary passages. The book of Esther is one story, a narrative, and we hope this helps the reader quickly identify where the action is happening in the main story thread.

Our final touch was to add a classic serif drop cap to the beginning of each chapter of Esther—one last nod to the storybook feel. We're suckers for a good drop cap, and their application in this biblical narrative felt just right. ◆

Table of Contents

KEY VERSE

"If you keep silent at this time, relief and deliverance will come to the Jewish people from another place, but you and your father's family will be destroyed. Who knows, perhaps you have come to your royal position for such a time as this." – Esther 4:14

ON THE TIMELINE:

The story of Esther is rooted in the historical account of King Ahasuerus, who ruled Persia from 486 to 465 B.C. Esther was made queen of Persia in approximately 479 B.C., Haman's plot to destroy the Jews occurred in 474 B.C., and the first celebration of Purim took place in 473 B.C. The events in Esther occurred before those of Ezra and Nehemiah, but after the Decree of Cyrus had allowed the Jews in exile to return to Jerusalem. Most likely the book was written in the fourth century B.C. with Mordecai as its author.

A LITTLE BACKGROUND:

Esther is a unique book. It never mentions God by name, although His presence is implied in Mordecai's allusion to divine providence (4:14). The book of Esther is tightly connected with specific historical events, yet it is also a piece of literature, a narrative with all of the literary features necessary to make a great story. Esther is unique in that its purposes are not always explicitly stated but are derived from the story as a whole.

MESSAGE & PURPOSE:

For the Jewish people scattered around the Persian Empire, the book of Esther was a story that gave encouragement and hope. It provided a model of how Jewish people could not only survive, but thrive in a Gentile environment. It displayed the work of God, evident but unseen, in the unfolding story of deliverance and redemption—making an orphan girl the queen and using her courage and influence to save the Jews from annihilation.

Cast of Characters

Ahasuerus

ESTHER 1:1

King of 127 provinces from India to Cush

Reigned in the fortress of Persia at Susa

Haman

ESTHER 3:1-11

King Ahasuerus's highest ranking official

Ordered all Jews to be destroyed after Mordecai refused to bow to him

Vashti

King Ahasuerus's wife

Banished from the king's presence because she refused to come when he called her

ESTHER 1:10-18

Memucan

One of King Ahasuerus's eunuchs

Advised the king to replace Vashti with a new wife

ESTHER 1:14, 16

Bigthan and Teresh

Two of King Ahasuerus's eunuchs who conspired to assassinate him

Exposed by Mordecai, who told Esther of their conspiracy

ESTHER 2:21-23

Esther

ESTHER 2:7-10

A young Jewish girl chosen by King Ahasuerus to replace Vashti as queen

Kept her Jewish heritage a secret, then used her status as queen to save her people

Mordecai

ESTHER 2:5-7, 3:2-6

Esther's cousin and guardian who advised her to keep her ethnicity and family background a secret

Refused to bow down to Haman

Hegai

One of King Ahasuerus's eunuchs

In charge of the women who were candidates to become the new queen

ESTHER 2:3

Hathach

The king's eunuch assigned to tend to Queen Esther

Carried messages between Esther and Mordecai

ESTHER 4:5-9

Zeresh

Haman's wife

Advised Haman to build 75-foot gallows on which to hang Mordecai

ESTHER 5:10, 14

Harbona

One of King Ahasuerus's eunuchs

Advised the king to hang Haman on Haman's own gallows

ESTHER 7:9

13

DAY 1:

Vashti Angers the King

ESTHER 1, PSALM 32:7, DANIEL 6:8, 13-18

1

VASHTI ANGERS THE KING

[1] These events took place during the days of Ahasuerus, who ruled 127 provinces from India to Cush. [2] In those days King Ahasuerus reigned from his royal throne in the fortress at Susa. [3] He held a feast in the third year of his reign for all his officials and staff, the army of Persia and Media, the nobles, and the officials from the provinces. [4] He displayed the glorious wealth of his kingdom and the magnificent splendor of his greatness for a total of 180 days.

[5] At the end of this time, the king held a week-long banquet in the garden courtyard of the royal palace for all the people, from the greatest to the least, who were present in the fortress of Susa. [6] White and violet linen hangings were fastened with fine white and purple linen cords to silver rods on marble columns. Gold and silver couches were arranged on a mosaic pavement of red feldspar, marble, mother-of-pearl, and precious stones.

[7] Drinks were served in an array of gold goblets, each with a different design. Royal wine flowed freely, according to the king's bounty. [8] The drinking was according to royal decree: "There are no restrictions." The king had ordered every wine steward in his household to serve whatever each person wanted. [9] Queen Vashti also gave a feast for the women of King Ahasuerus's palace.

[10] On the seventh day, when the king was feeling good from the wine, Ahasuerus commanded Mehuman, Biztha, Harbona, Bigtha, Abagtha, Zethar, and Carkas—the seven eunuchs who personally served him— [11] to bring Queen Vashti before him with her royal crown. He wanted to show off her beauty to the people and the officials, because she was very beautiful. [12] But Queen Vashti refused to come at the king's command that was delivered by his eunuchs. The king became furious and his anger burned within him.

THE KING'S DECREE

[13] The king consulted the wise men who understood the times, for it was his normal procedure to confer with experts in law and justice. [14] The most trusted ones were Carshena, Shethar, Admatha, Tarshish, Meres, Marsena, and Memucan. They were the seven officials of Persia and Media who had personal access to the king and occupied the highest positions in the kingdom. [15] The king asked, "According to the law, what should be done with Queen Vashti, since she refused to obey King Ahasuerus's command that was delivered by the eunuchs?"

[16] Memucan said in the presence of the king and his officials, "Queen Vashti has wronged not only the king, but all the officials and the peoples who are in every one of King Ahasuerus's provinces. [17] For the queen's action will become public knowledge to all the women and cause them to despise their husbands and say, 'King Ahasuerus ordered Queen Vashti brought before him, but she did not come.' [18] Before this day is over, the noble women of Persia and Media who hear about the queen's act will say the same thing to all the king's officials, resulting in more contempt and fury.

[19] "If it meets the king's approval, he should personally issue a royal decree. Let it be recorded in the laws of Persia and Media, so that it cannot be revoked: Vashti is not to enter King Ahasuerus's presence, and her royal position is to be given to another woman who is more worthy than she. [20] The decree the king issues will be heard throughout his vast kingdom, so all women will honor their husbands, from the greatest to the least."

[21] The king and his counselors approved the proposal, and he followed Memucan's advice. [22] He sent letters to all the royal provinces, to each province in its own script and to each ethnic group in its own language, that every man should be master of his own house and speak in the language of his own people.

continued

"What should be done
with Queen Vashti?"

ESTHER 1:15

continued

PSALM 32:7

You are my hiding place;
you protect me from trouble.
You surround me with joyful shouts of deliverance.   *Selah*

DANIEL 6:8, 13-18

[8] "Therefore, Your Majesty, establish the edict and sign the document so that, as a law of the Medes and Persians, it is irrevocable and cannot be changed."

…

[13] Then they replied to the king, "Daniel, one of the Judean exiles, has ignored you, the king, and the edict you signed, for he prays three times a day." [14] As soon as the king heard this, he was very displeased; he set his mind on rescuing Daniel and made every effort until sundown to deliver him.

[15] Then these men went together to the king and said to him, "You know, Your Majesty, that it is a law of the Medes and Persians that no edict or ordinance the king establishes can be changed."

[16] So the king gave the order, and they brought Daniel and threw him into the lions' den. The king said to Daniel, "May your God, whom you continually serve, rescue you!" [17] A stone was brought and placed over the mouth of the den. The king sealed it with his own signet ring and with the signet rings of his nobles, so that nothing in regard to Daniel could be changed. [18] Then the king went to his palace and spent the night fasting. No diversions were brought to him, and he could not sleep.

DAY 2:

The King Searches for a Queen

ESTHER 2, PROVERBS 31:10-31

2

THE SEARCH FOR A NEW QUEEN

[1] Some time later, when King Ahasuerus's rage had cooled down, he remembered Vashti, what she had done, and what was decided against her. [2] The king's personal attendants suggested, "Let a search be made for beautiful young virgins for the king. [3] Let the king appoint commissioners in each province of his kingdom, so that they may gather all the beautiful young virgins to the harem at the fortress of Susa. Put them under the supervision of Hegai, the king's eunuch, keeper of the women, and give them the required beauty treatments. [4] Then the young woman who pleases the king will become queen instead of Vashti." This suggestion pleased the king, and he did accordingly.

[5] In the fortress of Susa, there was a Jewish man named Mordecai son of Jair, son of Shimei, son of Kish, a Benjaminite. [6] He had been taken into exile from Jerusalem with the other captives when King Nebuchadnezzar of Babylon took King Jeconiah of Judah into exile. [7] Mordecai was the legal guardian of his cousin Hadassah (that is, Esther), because she had no father or mother. The young woman had a beautiful figure and was extremely good-looking. When her father and mother died, Mordecai had adopted her as his own daughter.

[8] When the king's command and edict became public knowledge and when many young women were gathered at the fortress of Susa under Hegai's supervision, Esther was taken to the palace, into the supervision of Hegai, keeper of the women. [9] The young woman pleased him and gained his favor so that he accelerated the process of the beauty treatments and the special diet that she received. He assigned seven hand-picked female servants to her from the palace and transferred her and her servants to the harem's best quarters.

[10] Esther did not reveal her ethnicity or her family background, because Mordecai had ordered her not to make them known. [11] Every day Mordecai took a walk in front of the harem's courtyard to learn how Esther was doing and to see what was happening to her.

[12] During the year before each young woman's turn to go to King Ahasuerus, the harem regulation required her to receive beauty treatments with oil of myrrh for six months and then with perfumes and cosmetics for another six months. [13] When the young woman would go to the king, she was given whatever she requested to take with her from the harem to the palace. [14] She would go in the evening, and in the morning she would return to a second harem under the supervision of the king's eunuch Shaashgaz, keeper of the concubines. She never went to the king again, unless he desired her and summoned her by name.

ESTHER BECOMES QUEEN

[15] Esther was the daughter of Abihail, the uncle of Mordecai who had adopted her as his own daughter. When her turn came to go to the king, she did not ask for anything except what Hegai, the king's eunuch, keeper of the women, suggested. Esther gained favor in the eyes of everyone who saw her.

[16] She was taken to King Ahasuerus in the palace in the tenth month, the month Tebeth, in the seventh year of his reign. [17] The king loved Esther more than all the other women. She won more favor and approval from him than did any of the other virgins. He placed the royal crown on her head and made her queen in place of Vashti. [18] The king held a great banquet for all his officials and staff. It was Esther's banquet. He freed his provinces from tax payments and gave gifts worthy of the king's bounty.

MORDECAI SAVES THE KING

[19] When the virgins were gathered a second time, Mordecai was sitting at the King's Gate. [20] (Esther had not revealed her family background or her ethnicity, as Mordecai had directed. She obeyed Mordecai's orders, as she always had while he raised her.)

[21] During those days while Mordecai was sitting at the King's Gate, Bigthan and Teresh, two of the king's eunuchs who guarded the entrance, became infuriated and planned to assassinate King Ahasuerus. [22] When Mordecai learned of the plot, he reported it to Queen Esther, and she told the king on Mordecai's behalf. [23] When the report was investigated and verified, both men were hanged on the gallows. This event was recorded in the Historical Record in the king's presence.

PROVERBS 31:10-31

IN PRAISE OF A WIFE OF NOBLE CHARACTER

[10] Who can find a wife of noble character?
She is far more precious than jewels.
[11] The heart of her husband trusts in her,
and he will not lack anything good.
[12] She rewards him with good, not evil,
all the days of her life.
[13] She selects wool and flax
and works with willing hands.
[14] She is like the merchant ships,
bringing her food from far away.
[15] She rises while it is still night
and provides food for her household
and portions for her female servants.
[16] She evaluates a field and buys it;
she plants a vineyard with her earnings.
[17] She draws on her strength
and reveals that her arms are strong.
[18] She sees that her profits are good,
and her lamp never goes out at night.
[19] She extends her hands to the spinning staff,
and her hands hold the spindle.
[20] Her hands reach out to the poor,
and she extends her hands to the needy.

[21] She is not afraid for her household when it snows,
for all in her household are doubly clothed.
[22] She makes her own bed coverings;
her clothing is fine linen and purple.
[23] Her husband is known at the city gates,
where he sits among the elders of the land.
[24] She makes and sells linen garments;
she delivers belts to the merchants.
[25] Strength and honor are her clothing,
and she can laugh at the time to come.
[26] Her mouth speaks wisdom,
and loving instruction is on her tongue.
[27] She watches over the activities of her household
and is never idle.
[28] Her children rise up and call her blessed;
her husband also praises her:
[29] "Many women have done noble deeds,
but you surpass them all!"
[30] Charm is deceptive and beauty is fleeting,
but a woman who fears the LORD will be praised.
[31] Give her the reward of her labor,
and let her works praise her at the city gates.

DAY 3:

Haman Plans to Kill the Jews

——

ESTHER 3, PSALM 68:20, PROVERBS 16:33

3

HAMAN'S PLAN TO KILL THE JEWS

[1] After all this took place, King Ahasuerus honored Haman, son of Hammedatha the Agagite. He promoted him in rank and gave him a higher position than all the other officials. [2] The entire royal staff at the King's Gate bowed down and paid homage to Haman, because the king had commanded this to be done for him. But Mordecai would not bow down or pay homage. [3] The members of the royal staff at the King's Gate asked Mordecai, "Why are you disobeying the king's command?" [4] When they had warned him day after day and he still would not listen to them, they told Haman in order to see if Mordecai's actions would be tolerated, since he had told them he was a Jew.

[5] When Haman saw that Mordecai was not bowing down or paying him homage, he was filled with rage. [6] And when he learned of Mordecai's ethnic identity, it seemed repugnant to Haman to do away with Mordecai alone. He planned to destroy all of Mordecai's people, the Jews, throughout Ahasuerus's kingdom.

[7] In the first month, the month of Nisan, in King Ahasuerus's twelfth year, the Pur—that is, the lot—was cast before Haman for each day in each month, and it fell on the twelfth month, the month Adar. [8] Then Haman informed King Ahasuerus, "There is one ethnic group, scattered throughout the peoples in every province of your kingdom, keeping themselves separate. Their laws are different from everyone else's and they do not obey the king's laws. It is not in the king's best interest to tolerate them. [9] If the king approves, let an order be drawn up authorizing their destruction, and I will pay 375 tons of silver to the officials for deposit in the royal treasury."

[10] The king removed his signet ring from his finger and gave it to Haman son of Hammedatha the Agagite, the enemy of the Jewish people. [11] Then the king told Haman, "The money and people are given to you to do with as you see fit."

[12] The royal scribes were summoned on the thirteenth day of the first month, and the order was written exactly as Haman commanded. It was intended for the royal satraps, the governors of each of the provinces, and the officials of each ethnic group and written for each province in its own script and to each ethnic group in its own language. It was written in the name of King Ahasuerus and sealed with the royal signet ring. [13] Letters were sent by couriers to each of the royal provinces telling the officials to destroy, kill, and annihilate all the Jewish people—young and old, women and children—and plunder their possessions on a single day, the thirteenth day of Adar, the twelfth month.

[14] A copy of the text, issued as law throughout every province, was distributed to all the peoples so that they might get ready for that day. [15] The couriers left, spurred on by royal command, and the law was issued in the fortress of Susa. The king and Haman sat down to drink, while the city of Susa was in confusion.

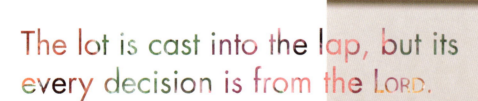

The lot is cast into the lap, but its every decision is from the Lord.

PROVERBS 16:33

PSALM 68:20

Our God is a God of salvation,
and escape from death belongs to the LORD my Lord.

PROVERBS 16:33

The lot is cast into the lap,
but its every decision is from the LORD.

Purim
AND THE OTHER OLD TESTAMENT
FEASTS FULFILLED IN CHRIST

In Esther 9:20-28, we find the origin of the Jewish feast known as Purim, or The Feast of Lots. This feast celebrated the Jewish people's deliverance from Haman's wicked plan to destroy them in Persia.

Purim, and the other Jewish feasts in the Old Testament, commemorate what it means for a people to belong to the Lord. The feasts helped God's people recall His faithfulness—a faithfulness ultimately fulfilled in Christ.

This chart provides a look at each of those feasts, what they celebrate, and how Christ fulfills them.

	WHEN	DESCRIPTION		FULFILLED IN CHRIST	
PURIM (FEAST OF LOTS)	ADAR 14 (FEB/MAR)	Commemorates how the Jewish people were delivered from Haman's plot to kill them in the days of Esther.	Est 9	We would have perished in our sin without Christ's intervention. Just as Esther represented her people by pleading their case before the Persian king, Jesus represents us before God.	Jn 3:16-17 2Co 1:9-11 2Tm 4:18 Heb 13:6
PASSOVER	NISAN 14-15 (MAR/APR)	Commemorates how God spared the firstborn sons of Israel in Egypt, accepting the blood of a lamb instead.	Ex 12:1-14 Lv 23:4-5	Christ, God's firstborn Son, became our Passover Lamb by dying in our place.	Jn 1:29 Jn 14:14-16 1Pt 1:18-19
FESTIVAL OF UNLEAVENED BREAD	NISAN 15-21 (MAR/APR)	Commemorates God's deliverance of Israel out of Egypt. In their haste to flee, they had no time to let their bread leaven.	Ex 12:39-42 Lv 23:6-8	Christ instituted the Lord's Supper on the eve of this feast, breaking bread and calling it His body, given for His people. During this feast, He was buried, like a seed waiting to bear the first fruit of salvation.	Mk 14:1 1Co 5:6-8
PENTECOST (FESTIVAL OF FIRST FRUITS)	SIVAN 6 (MAY/JUNE)	Commemorates the giving of the law at Mount Sinai. It was meant to be a guide for life, but because of sin, no one could live this life of obedience.	Ex 23:16 Ex 34:22 Lv 23:15-21	Christ's resurrection made Him the "firstfruits from the dead," the one who kept the law perfectly in our place. After His resurrection, He sent the Holy Spirit to live within His people and bear spiritual fruit in us.	Mt 28:1-10 Ac 2:1-4 1Co 15:20-23 2Th 2:13
ROSH HASHANAH (FESTIVAL OF TRUMPETS)	TISHRI 1 (SEPT/OCT)	Celebrates the beginning of a new year with the blowing of the trumpets. This feast reminded God's people of His faithful love for them.	Lv 23:23-25 Nm 10:9 Nm 29:1-6	The return of Christ will happen at the sound of a heavenly trumpet. That day will mark a new beginning as He ushers in His kingdom perfectly and completely.	Mt 24:30-31 1Co 15:51-52 1Th 4:16
YOM KIPPUR (DAY OF ATONEMENT)	TISHRI 10 (SEPT/OCT)	The day the high priest makes atonement for the nation's sin before God. The sins of the nation were symbolically placed on a goat which was cast out of the camp.	Ex 30:10 Lv 16:15-27 Lv 23:26-33	Jesus was led to a cross outside the city walls, like the goat cast outside of the camp. On the cross, He bore our sins, sanctifying us by His blood.	Is 53:1-12 Heb 13:11-12 Rv 13:8
SUKKOT (FESTIVAL OF TABERNACLES)	TISHRI 15-21 (SEPT/OCT)	Commemorates Israel's forty years of wilderness wandering. God dwelt among His people in a tabernacle, giving them manna and water.	Lv 23:33-43 Nm 29:12-39 Dt 16:13	Jesus is God who took on flesh and dwelled among us. He lived in the center of our world and gave us what we need to live in eternity.	Jn 1:10-14 1Co 10:4 Heb 9:1-11

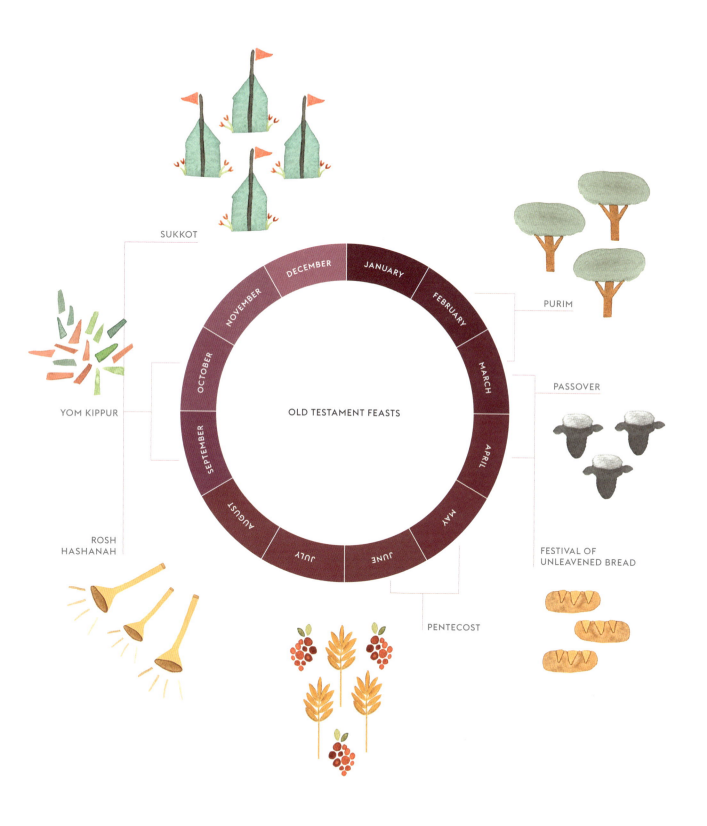

SUKKOT

PURIM

YOM KIPPUR

PASSOVER

ROSH HASHANAH

FESTIVAL OF UNLEAVENED BREAD

PENTECOST

OLD TESTAMENT FEASTS

DECEMBER
NOVEMBER
OCTOBER
SEPTEMBER
AUGUST
JULY
JUNE
MAY
APRIL
MARCH
FEBRUARY
JANUARY

DAY 4:

Mordecai Appeals to Esther

ESTHER 4, ISAIAH 15:1-3, ROMANS 5:6-11

4

MORDECAI APPEALS TO ESTHER

[1] When Mordecai learned all that had occurred, he tore his clothes, put on sackcloth and ashes, went into the middle of the city, and cried loudly and bitterly. [2] He went only as far as the King's Gate, since the law prohibited anyone wearing sackcloth from entering the King's Gate. [3] There was great mourning among the Jewish people in every province where the king's command and edict came. They fasted, wept, and lamented, and many lay in sackcloth and ashes.

[4] Esther's female servants and her eunuchs came and reported the news to her, and the queen was overcome with fear. She sent clothes for Mordecai to wear so that he would take off his sackcloth, but he did not accept them. [5] Esther summoned Hathach, one of the king's eunuchs who attended her, and dispatched him to Mordecai to learn what he was doing and why. [6] So Hathach went out to Mordecai in the city square in front of the King's Gate. [7] Mordecai told him everything that had happened as well as the exact amount of money Haman had promised to pay the royal treasury for the slaughter of the Jews.

[8] Mordecai also gave him a copy of the written decree issued in Susa ordering their destruction, so that Hathach might show it to Esther, explain it to her, and command her to approach the king, implore his favor, and plead with him personally for her people. [9] Hathach came and repeated Mordecai's response to Esther.

[10] Esther spoke to Hathach and commanded him to tell Mordecai, [11] "All the royal officials and the people of the royal provinces know that one law applies to every man or woman who approaches the king in the inner courtyard and who has not been summoned—the death penalty— unless the king extends the gold scepter, allowing that person to live. I have not been summoned to appear before the king for the last thirty days." [12] Esther's response was reported to Mordecai.

[13] Mordecai told the messenger to reply to Esther, "Don't think that you will escape the fate of all the Jews because you are in the king's palace. [14] If you keep silent at this time, relief and deliverance will come to the Jewish people from another place, but you and your father's family will be destroyed. Who knows, perhaps you have come to your royal position for such a time as this."

[15] Esther sent this reply to Mordecai: [16] "Go and assemble all the Jews who can be found in Susa and fast for me. Don't eat or drink for three days, night or day. I and my female servants will also fast in the same way. After that, I will go to the king even if it is against the law. If I perish, I perish." [17] So Mordecai went and did everything Esther had commanded him.

continued

"If I perish, I perish."

ESTHER 4:16

ISAIAH 15:1-3

A PRONOUNCEMENT AGAINST MOAB

[1] A pronouncement concerning Moab:

Ar in Moab is devastated,
destroyed in a night.
Kir in Moab is devastated,
destroyed in a night.
[2] Dibon went up to its temple
to weep at its high places.
Moab wails on Nebo and at Medeba.
Every head is shaved;
every beard is chopped short.
[3] In its streets they wear sackcloth;
on its rooftops and in its public squares everyone wails,
falling down and weeping.

ROMANS 5:6-11

THOSE DECLARED RIGHTEOUS ARE RECONCILED

[6] For while we were still helpless, at the right time, Christ died for the ungodly. [7] For rarely will someone die for a just person—though for a good person perhaps someone might even dare to die. [8] But God proves his own love for us in that while we were still sinners, Christ died for us. [9] How much more then, since we have now been declared righteous by his blood, will we be saved through him from wrath. [10] For if, while we were enemies, we were reconciled to God through the death of his Son, then how much more, having been reconciled, will we be saved by his life. [11] And not only that, but we also rejoice in God through our Lord Jesus Christ, through whom we have now received this reconciliation.

NOTES

DAY 5:

Esther Approaches the King

ESTHER 5, MARK 6:14-29, PROVERBS 16:18

5

ESTHER APPROACHES THE KING

[1] On the third day, Esther dressed in her royal clothing and stood in the inner courtyard of the palace facing it. The king was sitting on his royal throne in the royal courtroom, facing its entrance. [2] As soon as the king saw Queen Esther standing in the courtyard, she gained favor in his eyes. The king extended the gold scepter in his hand toward Esther, and she approached and touched the tip of the scepter.

[3] "What is it, Queen Esther?" the king asked her. "Whatever you want, even to half the kingdom, will be given to you."

[4] "If it pleases the king," Esther replied, "may the king and Haman come today to the banquet I have prepared for them."

[5] The king said, "Hurry, and get Haman so we can do as Esther has requested." So the king and Haman went to the banquet Esther had prepared.

[6] While drinking the wine, the king asked Esther, "Whatever you ask will be given to you. Whatever you want, even to half the kingdom, will be done."

[7] Esther answered, "This is my petition and my request: [8] If I have found favor in the eyes of the king, and if it pleases the king to grant my petition and perform my request, may the king and Haman come to the banquet I will prepare for them. Tomorrow I will do what the king has asked."

[9] That day Haman left full of joy and in good spirits. But when Haman saw Mordecai at the King's Gate, and Mordecai didn't rise or tremble in fear at his presence, Haman was filled with rage toward Mordecai. [10] Yet Haman controlled himself and went home. He sent for his friends and his wife Zeresh to join him. [11] Then Haman described for them his glorious wealth and his many sons. He told them all how the king had honored him and promoted him in rank over the other officials and the royal staff. [12] "What's more," Haman added, "Queen Esther invited no one but me to join the king at the banquet she had prepared. I am invited again tomorrow to join her with the king. [13] Still, none of this satisfies me since I see Mordecai the Jew sitting at the King's Gate all the time."

[14] His wife Zeresh and all his friends told him, "Have them build a gallows seventy-five feet tall. Ask the king in the morning to hang Mordecai on it. Then go to the banquet with the king and enjoy yourself." The advice pleased Haman, so he had the gallows constructed.

continued

Pride comes before destruction,
and an arrogant spirit before a fall.

PROVERBS 16:18

MARK 6:14-29

JOHN THE BAPTIST BEHEADED

¹⁴ King Herod heard about it, because Jesus's name had become well known. Some said, "John the Baptist has been raised from the dead, and that's why miraculous powers are at work in him." ¹⁵ But others said, "He's Elijah." Still others said, "He's a prophet, like one of the prophets from long ago."

¹⁶ When Herod heard of it, he said, "John, the one I beheaded, has been raised!"

¹⁷ For Herod himself had given orders to arrest John and to chain him in prison on account of Herodias, his brother Philip's wife, because he had married her. ¹⁸ John had been telling Herod, "It is not lawful for you to have your brother's wife." ¹⁹ So Herodias held a grudge against him and wanted to kill him. But she could not, ²⁰ because Herod feared John and protected him, knowing he was a righteous and holy man. When Herod heard him he would be very perplexed, and yet he liked to listen to him.

²¹ An opportune time came on his birthday, when Herod gave a banquet for his nobles, military commanders, and the leading men of Galilee. ²² When Herodias's own daughter came in and danced, she pleased Herod and his guests. The king said to the girl, "Ask me whatever you want, and I'll give it to you." ²³ He promised her with an oath: "Whatever you ask me I will give you, up to half my kingdom."

²⁴ She went out and said to her mother, "What should I ask for?"

"John the Baptist's head," she said.

²⁵ At once she hurried to the king and said, "I want you to give me John the Baptist's head on a platter immediately." ²⁶ Although the king was deeply distressed, because of his oaths and the guests he did not want to refuse her. ²⁷ The king immediately sent for an executioner and commanded him to bring John's head. So he went and beheaded him in prison, ²⁸ brought his head on a platter, and gave it to the girl. Then the girl gave it to her mother. ²⁹ When John's disciples heard about it, they came and removed his corpse and placed it in a tomb.

PROVERBS 16:18

Pride comes before destruction,
and an arrogant spirit before a fall.

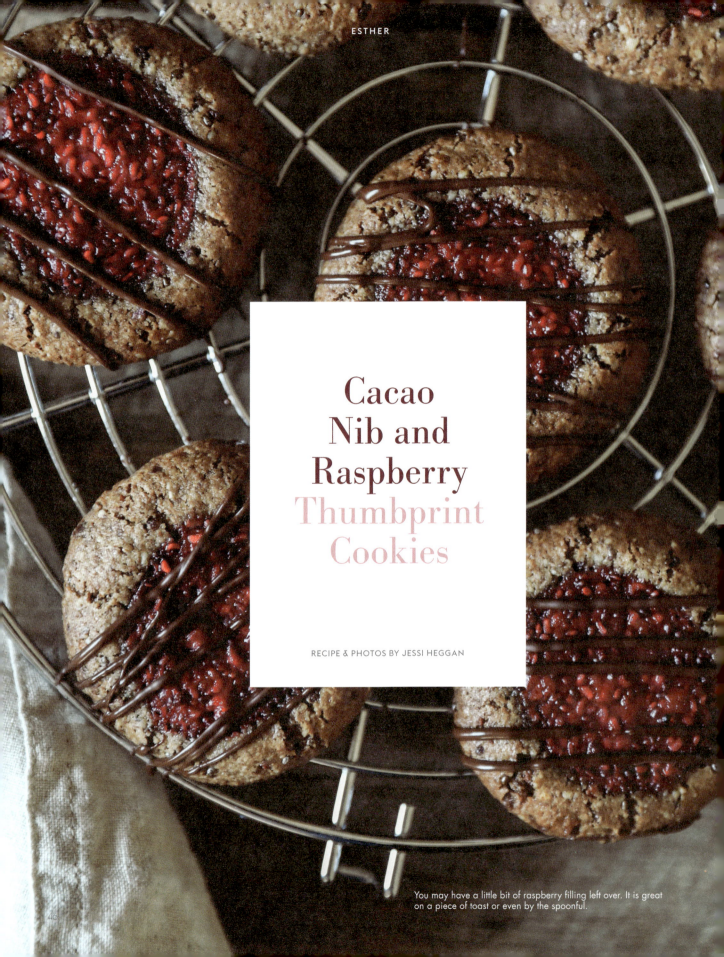

Cacao Nib and Raspberry Thumbprint Cookies

RECIPE & PHOTOS BY JESSI HEGGAN

You may have a little bit of raspberry filling left over. It is great on a piece of toast or even by the spoonful.

YIELDS 12-14 COOKIES

CACAO NIB COOKIE
2 cups pecan halves
½ cup cacao nibs
1 tbsp chia seeds
½ tsp baking soda
¼ tsp sea salt
¼ cup maple syrup

RASPBERRY FILLING
1½ cups frozen raspberry
1 tsp vanilla
3 tsp chia seeds

CHOCOLATE DRIZZLE
2 ounces dark chocolate, melted

INSTRUCTIONS

Preheat oven to 350° and line a baking sheet with parchment paper.

Heat a small saucepan to medium heat, then add the frozen raspberry, vanilla, and chia seeds and cook until mixture resembles jam and is slightly thickened—approximately 8-10 minutes. Remove from heat and let cool to room temperature.

Add the pecans, cacao nibs, chia seeds, baking soda, and salt to a food processor and pulse for 10-15 seconds, or until everything is coarsely chopped. Add the maple syrup and pulse until the dough starts to become one unit.

Scoop out a tablespoon of dough and roll it into a ball. Place on the baking sheet. Use your thumb to make an imprint in the middle of the cookie. Repeat with the remaining dough.

Cook for 5 minutes, then remove from oven. You may need to use your thumb to make an imprint again after the dough rises in the oven.

Scoop about 1-2 teaspoons of raspberry filling into the middle of the cookie. Repeat until all cookies are filled.

Bake for another 7-9 minutes, then remove from oven and let cool. Drizzle with melted chocolate.

Cookies can be stored in an airtight container 2-3 days.

DAY 6: GRACE DAY

YOU ARE MY HIDING PLACE;
YOU PROTECT ME FROM TROUBLE.
YOU SURROUND ME WITH JOYFUL
SHOUTS OF DELIVERANCE.

PSALM 32:7

Take this day as an opportunity
to catch up on your reading,
pray, and rest in the presence
of the Lord.

DAY 7: WEEKLY TRUTH

"If you keep silent at this time, relief and deliverance will come to the Jewish people from another place, but you and your father's family will be destroyed."

ESTHER 4:14a

Memorizing Scripture is one of the best ways to carry God-breathed truth, instruction, and reproof wherever we go.

As we read through the book of Esther, we will memorize the book's key verse in two parts. We'll begin with the first part of the verse—a reminder that God's sovereignty does not depend on us.

DAY 8:

The King Honors Mordecai

ESTHER 6, PROVERBS 26:27, ISAIAH 52:1-2

6

MORDECAI HONORED BY THE KING

[1] That night sleep escaped the king, so he ordered the book recording daily events to be brought and read to the king. [2] They found the written report of how Mordecai had informed on Bigthana and Teresh, two of the king's eunuchs who guarded the entrance, when they planned to assassinate King Ahasuerus. [3] The king inquired, "What honor and special recognition have been given to Mordecai for this act?"

The king's personal attendants replied, "Nothing has been done for him."

[4] The king asked, "Who is in the court?" Now Haman was just entering the outer court of the palace to ask the king to hang Mordecai on the gallows he had prepared for him.

[5] The king's attendants answered him, "Haman is there, standing in the court."

"Have him enter," the king ordered. [6] Haman entered, and the king asked him, "What should be done for the man the king wants to honor?"

Haman thought to himself, "Who is it the king would want to honor more than me?" [7] Haman told the king, "For the man the king wants to honor: [8] Have them bring a royal garment that the king himself has worn and a horse the king himself has ridden, which has a royal crown on its head. [9] Put the garment and the horse under the charge of one of the king's most noble officials. Have them clothe the man the king wants to honor, parade him on the horse through the city square, and proclaim before him, 'This is what is done for the man the king wants to honor.'"

[10] The king told Haman, "Hurry, and do just as you proposed. Take a garment and a horse for Mordecai the Jew, who is sitting at the King's Gate. Do not leave out anything you have suggested."

[11] So Haman took the garment and the horse. He clothed Mordecai and paraded him through the city square, crying out before him, "This is what is done for the man the king wants to honor."

[12] Then Mordecai returned to the King's Gate, but Haman hurried off for home, mournful and with his head covered. [13] Haman told his wife Zeresh and all his friends everything that had happened. His advisers and his wife Zeresh said to him, "Since Mordecai is Jewish, and you have begun to fall before him, you won't overcome him, because your downfall is certain." [14] While they were still speaking with him, the king's eunuchs arrived and rushed Haman to the banquet Esther had prepared.

The one who digs a pit will fall into it.

PROVERBS 26:27

continued

PROVERBS 26:27

The one who digs a pit will fall into it,
and whoever rolls a stone—
it will come back on him.

ISAIAH 52:1-2

[1] Wake up, wake up;
put on your strength, Zion!
Put on your beautiful garments,
Jerusalem, the Holy City!
For the uncircumcised and the unclean
will no longer enter you.
[2] Stand up, shake the dust off yourself!
Take your seat, Jerusalem.
Remove the bonds from your neck,
captive Daughter Zion.

DAY 9:

The King Executes Haman

ESTHER 7, PSALM 91:2-3, REVELATION 20:11-15

7

HAMAN IS EXECUTED

[1] The king and Haman came to feast with Esther the queen. [2] Once again, on the second day while drinking wine, the king asked Esther, "Queen Esther, whatever you ask will be given to you. Whatever you seek, even to half the kingdom, will be done."

[3] Queen Esther answered, "If I have found favor in your eyes, Your Majesty, and if the king is pleased, spare my life; this is my request. And spare my people; this is my desire. [4] For my people and I have been sold to destruction, death, and extermination. If we had merely been sold as male and female slaves, I would have kept silent. Indeed, the trouble wouldn't be worth burdening the king."

[5] King Ahasuerus spoke up and asked Queen Esther, "Who is this, and where is the one who would devise such a scheme?"

[6] Esther answered, "The adversary and enemy is this evil Haman."

Haman stood terrified before the king and queen. [7] The king arose in anger and went from where they were drinking wine to the palace garden. Haman remained to beg Queen Esther for his life because he realized the king was planning something terrible for him. [8] Just as the king returned from the palace garden to the banquet hall, Haman was falling on the couch where Esther was reclining. The king exclaimed, "Would he actually violate the queen while I am in the house?" As soon as the statement left the king's mouth, they covered Haman's face.

[9] Harbona, one of the king's eunuchs, said: "There is a gallows seventy-five feet tall at Haman's house that he made for Mordecai, who gave the report that saved the king."

The king said, "Hang him on it."

[10] They hanged Haman on the gallows he had prepared for Mordecai. Then the king's anger subsided.

continued

PSALM 91:2-3

2 I will say concerning the LORD, who is my refuge and my fortress,
my God in whom I trust:
3 He himself will rescue you from the bird trap,
from the destructive plague.

REVELATION 20:11-15

THE GREAT WHITE THRONE JUDGMENT

11 Then I saw a great white throne and one seated on it. Earth and heaven fled from his presence, and no place was found for them. 12 I also saw the dead, the great and the small, standing before the throne, and books were opened. Another book was opened, which is the book of life, and the dead were judged according to their works by what was written in the books. 13 Then the sea gave up the dead that were in it, and death and Hades gave up the dead that were in them; each one was judged according to their works. 14 Death and Hades were thrown into the lake of fire. This is the second death, the lake of fire. 15 And anyone whose name was not found written in the book of life was thrown into the lake of fire.

NOTES

DAY 10:

Esther Intervenes for the Jews

ESTHER 8, ROMANS 8:10-11, COLOSSIANS 3:1-4

8

ESTHER INTERVENES FOR THE JEWS

¹ That same day King Ahasuerus awarded Queen Esther the estate of Haman, the enemy of the Jews. Mordecai entered the king's presence because Esther had revealed her relationship to Mordecai. ² The king removed his signet ring he had recovered from Haman and gave it to Mordecai, and Esther put him in charge of Haman's estate.

³ Then Esther addressed the king again. She fell at his feet, wept, and begged him to revoke the evil of Haman the Agagite and his plot he had devised against the Jews. ⁴ The king extended the gold scepter toward Esther, so she got up and stood before the king.

⁵ She said, "If it pleases the king and I have found favor before him, if the matter seems right to the king and I am pleasing in his eyes, let a royal edict be written. Let it revoke the documents the scheming Haman son of Hammedatha the Agagite wrote to destroy the Jews who are in all the king's provinces. ⁶ For how could I bear to see the disaster that would come on my people? How could I bear to see the destruction of my relatives?"

⁷ King Ahasuerus said to Esther the queen and to Mordecai the Jew, "Look, I have given Haman's estate to Esther, and he was hanged on the gallows because he attacked the Jews. ⁸ Write in the king's name whatever pleases you concerning the Jews, and seal it with the royal signet ring. A document written in the king's name and sealed with the royal signet ring cannot be revoked."

⁹ On the twenty-third day of the third month —that is, the month Sivan—the royal scribes were summoned. Everything was written exactly as Mordecai commanded for the Jews, to the satraps, the governors, and the officials of the 127 provinces from India to Cush. The edict was written for each province in its own script, for each ethnic group in its own language, and to the Jews in their own script and language.

¹⁰ Mordecai wrote in King Ahasuerus's name and sealed the edicts with the royal signet ring. He sent the documents by mounted couriers, who rode fast horses bred in the royal stables.

¹¹ The king's edict gave the Jews in each and every city the right to assemble and defend themselves, to destroy, kill, and annihilate every ethnic and provincial army hostile to them, including women and children, and to take their possessions as spoils of war. ¹² This would take place on a single day throughout all the provinces of King Ahasuerus, on the thirteenth day of the twelfth month, the month Adar.

¹³ A copy of the text, issued as law throughout every province, was distributed to all the peoples so the Jews could be ready to avenge themselves against their enemies on that day. ¹⁴ The couriers rode out in haste on their royal horses at the king's urgent command. The law was also issued in the fortress of Susa.

¹⁵ Mordecai went from the king's presence clothed in royal purple and white, with a great gold crown and a purple robe of fine linen. The city of Susa shouted and rejoiced, ¹⁶ and the Jews celebrated with gladness, joy, and honor. ¹⁷ In every province and every city, wherever the king's command and his law reached, joy and rejoicing took place among the Jews. There was a celebration and a holiday. And many of the ethnic groups of the land professed themselves to be Jews because fear of the Jews had overcome them.

continued

THE BOOK OF

Esther

A Brief Timeline

483 BC — Ahasuerus kicks off his 180-day feast

Queen Vashti is dethroned

479 BC — Esther becomes queen of Persia

478 BC — Mordecai thwarts Bigthan and Teresh's conspiracy to kill King Ahasuerus

474 BC — Mordecai refuses to bow to Haman

Haman issues a royal decree for the annihilation of the Jews in the Persian Empire

Esther intercedes with King Ahasuerus on behalf of her people

King Ahasuerus honors Mordecai and has Haman hanged

473 BC — Celebration of Purim begins

472 BC — King Ahasuerus promotes Mordecai to second in command

ROMANS 8:10-11

[10] Now if Christ is in you, the body is dead because of sin, but the Spirit gives life because of righteousness. [11] And if the Spirit of him who raised Jesus from the dead lives in you, then he who raised Christ from the dead will also bring your mortal bodies to life through his Spirit who lives in you.

COLOSSIANS 3:1-4

THE LIFE OF THE NEW MAN

[1] So if you have been raised with Christ, seek the things above, where Christ is, seated at the right hand of God. [2] Set your minds on things above, not on earthly things. [3] For you died, and your life is hidden with Christ in God. [4] When Christ, who is your life, appears, then you also will appear with him in glory.

NOTES

DAY 11:

Esther's People Are Saved

———

ESTHER 9:1-22, NEHEMIAH 8:10, LUKE 1:46-55

9

VICTORIES OF THE JEWS

[1] The king's command and law went into effect on the thirteenth day of the twelfth month, the month Adar. On the day when the Jews' enemies had hoped to overpower them, just the opposite happened. The Jews overpowered those who hated them. [2] In each of King Ahasuerus's provinces the Jews assembled in their cities to attack those who intended to harm them. Not a single person could withstand them; fear of them fell on every nationality.

[3] All the officials of the provinces, the satraps, the governors, and the royal civil administrators aided the Jews because they feared Mordecai. [4] For Mordecai exercised great power in the palace, and his fame spread throughout the provinces as he became more and more powerful.

[5] The Jews put all their enemies to the sword, killing and destroying them. They did what they pleased to those who hated them. [6] In the fortress of Susa the Jews killed and destroyed five hundred men, [7] including Parshandatha, Dalphon, Aspatha, [8] Poratha, Adalia, Aridatha, [9] Parmashta, Arisai, Aridai, and Vaizatha. [10] They killed these ten sons of Haman son of Hammedatha, the enemy of the Jews. However, they did not seize any plunder.

[11] On that day the number of people killed in the fortress of Susa was reported to the king. [12] The king said to Queen Esther, "In the fortress of Susa the Jews have killed and destroyed five hundred men, including Haman's ten sons. What have they done in the rest of the royal provinces? Whatever you ask will be given to you. Whatever you seek will also be done."

[13] Esther answered, "If it pleases the king, may the Jews who are in Susa also have tomorrow to carry out today's law, and may the bodies of Haman's ten sons be hung on the gallows." [14] The king gave the orders for this to be done, so a law was announced in Susa, and they hung the bodies of Haman's ten sons. [15] The Jews in Susa assembled again on the fourteenth day of the month of Adar and killed three hundred men in Susa, but they did not seize any plunder.

[16] The rest of the Jews in the royal provinces assembled, defended themselves, and gained relief from their enemies. They killed seventy-five thousand of those who hated them, but they did not seize any plunder. [17] They fought on the thirteenth day of the month of Adar and rested on the fourteenth, and it became a day of feasting and rejoicing.

[18] But the Jews in Susa had assembled on the thirteenth and the fourteenth days of the month. They rested on the fifteenth day of the month, and it became a day of feasting and rejoicing. [19] This explains why the rural Jews who live in villages observe the fourteenth day of the month of Adar as a time of rejoicing and feasting. It is a holiday when they send gifts to one another.

[20] Mordecai recorded these events and sent letters to all the Jews in all of King Ahasuerus's provinces, both near and far. [21] He ordered them to celebrate the fourteenth and fifteenth days of the month of Adar every year [22] because during those days the Jews gained relief from their enemies. That was the month when their sorrow was turned into rejoicing and their mourning into a holiday. They were to be days of feasting, rejoicing, and of sending gifts to one another and to the poor.

continued

That was the month when their
sorrow was turned into rejoicing
and their mourning into a holiday.

ESTHER 9:22

NEHEMIAH 8:10

Then he said to them, "Go and eat what is rich, drink what is sweet, and send portions to those who have nothing prepared, since today is holy to our Lord. Do not grieve, because the joy of the Lord is your strength."

LUKE 1:46-55

MARY'S PRAISE

[46] And Mary said:

My soul praises the greatness of the Lord,
[47] and my spirit rejoices in God my Savior,
[48] because he has looked with favor
on the humble condition of his servant.
Surely, from now on all generations
will call me blessed,
[49] because the Mighty One
has done great things for me,
and his name is holy.
[50] His mercy is from generation to generation
on those who fear him.
[51] He has done a mighty deed with his arm;
he has scattered the proud
because of the thoughts of their hearts;
[52] he has toppled the mighty from their thrones
and exalted the lowly.
[53] He has satisfied the hungry with good things
and sent the rich away empty.
[54] He has helped his servant Israel,
remembering his mercy
[55] to Abraham and his descendants forever,
just as he spoke to our ancestors.

A Kingdom Upside Down

REVERSALS IN ESTHER

God has chosen what is foolish in the world to shame the wise, and God has chosen what is weak in the world to shame the strong. God has chosen what is insignificant and despised in the world—what is viewed as nothing—to bring to nothing what is viewed as something, so that no one may boast in his presence. - 1 Corinthians 1:27-28

The book of Esther is a living picture of these words from Paul to the Corinthians. It is a book filled with reversals of fortune. Powerless people are rescued from evil rulers. The lowly are delivered from wicked plans. No one in this book boasts in their own glory without being humbled. Conversely, the humble are exalted.

1	THE TWO FACES OF THE KING	King Ahasuerus is introduced as powerful, extravagant, merry, and pompous. (1:1-8)
2	THE TWO QUEENS	Vashti fails to appear when summoned by her king. (1:12)
3	ESTHER'S PLACE IN THE WORLD	Esther is introduced as an orphan under the care of her cousin Mordecai. (2:5-7)
4	MORDECAI'S FATE	Haman makes plans to execute Mordecai because of his character. (3:2-5, 5:14)
5	HAMAN'S GALLOWS	Haman builds a gallows on which to hang Mordecai. (5:9-14)
6	BOWING THE KNEE	Haman demands that Mordecai bow down before him in worship. (3:1-2)
7	HAMAN'S ANNIHILATION	Haman wants to destroy the Jewish population in Persia. (3:8-11)

REVERSAL	**The king is embarrassed and angered when Vashti refuses to come to him.** (1:12)
REVERSAL	**Esther appears before the king, uninvited.** (8:3)
REVERSAL	**Esther becomes the queen of Persia.** (2:15-18)
REVERSAL	**The king honors Mordecai for his character.** (8:15)
REVERSAL	**The king has Haman hanged for treachery on the gallows Haman built.** (7:10)
REVERSAL	**Haman bows before Esther, pleading for mercy.** (7:7-8)
REVERSAL	**After Haman is put to death, his house is given to Jews—Esther and Mordecai.** (8:1-2)

DAY 12:

God's People Remember and Celebrate

—

ESTHER 9:23-32, ESTHER 10, LEVITICUS 16:29-31, EPHESIANS 1:3-14

9

ESTHER 9:23-32

[23] So the Jews agreed to continue the practice they had begun, as Mordecai had written them to do. [24] For Haman son of Hammedatha the Agagite, the enemy of all the Jews, had plotted against the Jews to destroy them. He cast the Pur—that is, the lot—to crush and destroy them. [25] But when the matter was brought before the king, he commanded by letter that the evil plan Haman had devised against the Jews return on his own head and that he should be hanged with his sons on the gallows. [26] For this reason these days are called Purim, from the word Pur. Because of all the instructions in this letter as well as what they had witnessed and what had happened to them, [27] the Jews bound themselves, their descendants, and all who joined with them to a commitment that they would not fail to celebrate these two days each and every year according to the written instructions and according to the time appointed. [28] These days are remembered and celebrated by every generation, family, province, and city, so that these days of Purim will not lose their significance in Jewish life and their memory will not fade from their descendants.

[29] Queen Esther, daughter of Abihail, along with Mordecai the Jew, wrote this second letter with full authority to confirm the letter about Purim. [30] He sent letters with assurances of peace and security to all the Jews who were in the 127 provinces of the kingdom of Ahasuerus, [31] in order to confirm these days of Purim at their proper time just as Mordecai the Jew and Esther the queen had established them and just as they had committed themselves and their descendants to the practices of fasting and lamentation. [32] So Esther's command confirmed these customs of Purim, which were then written into the record.

10

MORDECAI'S FAME

[1] King Ahasuerus imposed a tax throughout the land even to the farthest shores. [2] All of his powerful and magnificent accomplishments and the detailed account of Mordecai's great rank with which the king had honored him, have they not been written in the Book of the Historical Events of the Kings of Media and Persia? [3] Mordecai the Jew was second only to King Ahasuerus. He was famous among the Jews and highly esteemed by many of his relatives. He continued to pursue prosperity for his people and to speak for the well-being of all his descendants.

continued

These days are remembered and celebrated by every generation...

ESTHER 9:28

LEVITICUS 16:29-31

²⁹ This is to be a permanent statute for you: In the seventh month, on the tenth day of the month you are to practice self-denial and do no work, both the native and the alien who resides among you. ³⁰ Atonement will be made for you on this day to cleanse you, and you will be clean from all your sins before the LORD. ³¹ It is a Sabbath of complete rest for you, and you must practice self-denial; it is a permanent statute.

EPHESIANS 1:3-14

GOD'S RICH BLESSINGS

³ Blessed is the God and Father of our Lord Jesus Christ, who has blessed us with every spiritual blessing in the heavens in Christ. ⁴ For he chose us in him, before the foundation of the world, to be holy and blameless in love before him. ⁵ He predestined us to be adopted as sons through Jesus Christ for himself, according to the good pleasure of his will, ⁶ to the praise of his glorious grace that he lavished on us in the Beloved One.

⁷ In him we have redemption through his blood, the forgiveness of our trespasses, according to the riches of his grace ⁸ that he richly poured out on us with all wisdom and understanding. ⁹ He made known to us the mystery of his will, according to his good pleasure that he purposed in Christ ¹⁰ as a plan for the right time—to bring everything together in Christ, both things in heaven and things on earth in him.

¹¹ In him we have also received an inheritance, because we were predestined according to the plan of the one who works out everything in agreement with the purpose of his will, ¹² so that we who had already put our hope in Christ might bring praise to his glory.

¹³ In him you also were sealed with the promised Holy Spirit when you heard the word of truth, the gospel of your salvation, and when you believed. ¹⁴ The Holy Spirit is the down payment of our inheritance, until the redemption of the possession, to the praise of his glory.

NOTES

DAY 13: GRACE DAY

HE MADE KNOWN TO US THE MYSTERY OF HIS WILL,
ACCORDING TO HIS GOOD PLEASURE THAT HE
PURPOSED IN CHRIST AS A PLAN FOR THE RIGHT TIME—
TO BRING EVERYTHING TOGETHER IN CHRIST, BOTH
THINGS IN HEAVEN AND THINGS ON EARTH IN HIM.

EPHESIANS 1:9-10

Take this day as an opportunity
to catch up on your reading,
pray, and rest in the presence
of the Lord.

DAY 14: WEEKLY TRUTH

"Who knows,
perhaps you have come
to your royal position for
such a time as this."

ESTHER 4:14b

Memorizing Scripture is one
of the best ways to carry God-
breathed truth, instruction, and
reproof wherever we go.

As we read through the book of
Esther, we are memorizing the
book's key verse in two parts.
This week, we'll memorize the
end of the verse, which reminds
us that God has a purpose for
our lives.

GIVE THANKS
FOR THE BOOK OF ESTHER

—

The book of Esther is good news because it teaches us about God's providence. God's promise to give the Jews an eternal ruler remained in place, even in the face of threatened annihilation. Without ever mentioning Him by name, the book of Esther underscores the Lord's presence and sovereignty in the lives of His people. God's invisible hand was always at work in the story of Esther and her people, securing their deliverance even before man sought to devise their destruction.

Immortal, Invisible, God Only Wise

1 Immortal, invisible, God only wise,
2 Unresting, unhasting, and silent as light,
3 To all life Thou givest, to both great and small;
4 Great Father of glory, pure Father of light,

in light inaccessible hid from our eyes,
nor wanting nor wasting, Thou rulest in might;
in all life Thou livest, the true life of all;
Thine angels adore Thee, all veiling their sight;

most blessed, most glorious, the Ancient of Days,
Thy justice like mountains high soaring above,
we blossom and flourish as leaves on the tree,
all praise we would render, O help us to see

almighty, victorious, Thy great name we praise.
Thy clouds, which are fountains of goodness and love.
and wither and perish— but nought changest Thee.
'tis only the splendor of light hideth Thee.

Text: Walter Chalmers Smith (1824-1908), alt
Tune: *Welsh Melody*; harm. John Roberts (1822-1877)

Where did I study?

- ○ HOME
- ○ CHURCH
- ○ OFFICE
- ○ A FRIEND'S HOUSE
- ○ COFFEE SHOP
- ○ OTHER

DID I LISTEN TO MUSIC?

ARTIST:

SONG:

SCRIPTURE I WILL
SHARE WITH A FRIEND:

WHEN DID I HAVE MY BEST STUDYING SUCCESS?

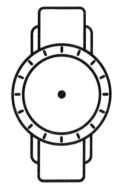

WHAT WAS HAPPENING IN THE WORLD?

What was my best takeaway?

WHAT WAS MY BIGGEST FEAR?   ▷   What was my greatest comfort?

_____

_____

_____

_____

_____

I LEARNED THESE UNEXPECTED NEW THINGS:

1

2

3

END DATE

| MONTH | DAY | YEAR |

COLOPHON

This book was printed offset in Nashville, Tennessee, on 70# Lynx Opaque. Typefaces used include Bodoni, Garamond, and Euclid. Cover is printed offset on Tango 15 pt C1S with a soft-touch matte laminate. Finished size is 8"x10".

EDITORS-IN-CHIEF: Raechel Myers and Amanda Bible Williams

CONTENT DIRECTOR: Russ Ramsey, MDiv., ThM.

EDITORS: Rebecca Faires and Kara Gause

EDITORIAL ASSISTANT: Ellen Taylor

ADDITIONAL THEOLOGICAL OVERSIGHT: Nate Shurden, MDiv.

CREATIVE DIRECTOR: Ryan Myers

ART DIRECTOR: Amanda Barnhart

DESIGNER: Kelsea Allen

LETTERER: Naomi Scheel

COVER & INTERIOR ILLUSTRATOR: Amanda Christine Estrada

PHOTOGRAPHERS: Michelle Mock, Mackenzie Kern,
Hannah Wenger, and Jessi Heggan

SUBSCRIPTION INQUIRIES:
orders@shereadstruth.com

She Reads Truth is a worldwide community of women who read God's Word together every day.

Founded in 2012, She Reads Truth invites women of all ages to engage with Scripture through daily reading plans, online conversation led by a vibrant community of contributors, and offline resources created at the intersection of beauty, goodness, and Truth.

STOP BY

shereadstruth.com

SHOP

shopshereadstruth.com

KEEP IN TOUCH

@shereadstruth

DOWNLOAD THE APP

SEND A NOTE

hello@shereadstruth.com

CONNECT

#SheReadsTruth

"WE NEED NEVER SHOUT ACROSS THE SPACES TO AN ABSENT GOD. HE IS NEARER THAN OUR OWN SOUL, CLOSER THAN OUR MOST SECRET THOUGHTS." —A.W. TOZER